Brazos, Carry Me

Brazos, Carry Me

Poems by Pablo Miguel Martínez

Foreword by Alicia Gaspar de Alba

Kórima Press

Cover Art: Karen Davis
Title: "Tom Walks Alone," from the "The McCann Family" series
Medium: Photograph
Date: 2013
www.yesthatkarendavis.com

Author Photograph: Amada Chávez Núñez

Book Design: Lorenzo Herrera y Lozano

Published by Kórima Press
San Francisco, CA
www.korimapress.com

ISBN:0615781683

For my father, Pablo Martínez, y a la memoria de mi mamá,
Blanca Perales Martínez, and for Hank, beautiful lamplighter of my soul

Contents

II. Brown Angel Pharmacy

Foreword

by Alicia Gaspar de Alba

There's something about growing up in Texas that breaks your heart. Whether it's El Paso, which is my hometown, or San Antonio, where Pablo Miguel Martínez was born and raised, whether it's Hargill or Houston, something about Texas—the sky, the light, the memory of the dispossessed—presses incessantly on your chest and cracks the shell of your heart. Perhaps, as Pablo writes in "This Valley," it's the ghosts.

> This valley is filled with ghosts
> miraculous multitudes ...
> whose phantom feet memorize
> labyrinths of lettuce, beet and grape

It's that phantom essence—the fecundity of the land mixed with the deep lyrical sorrow of all its losses—that lives and moves through these poems.

Brazos, Carry Me, as the title of the book suggests, is a paean to Texas, signified by the river Brazos, once named el Río de los Brazos de Dios by the Spaniards who conquered the northern province in the 16th century, for the majesty and length of that river could almost rival the arms of God. Indeed, it was at the Brazos River where the first rupture that became the U.S.-Mexican War (1846-1848) took place, as Mexican soldiers were slaughtered on their own land while President James Polk declared to Congress that "American blood has been shed on American soil," thus justifying the U.S. invasion of Mexico. It is this battle and this river that Brazos Street in San Antonio commemorates, and the reenactment of that takeover that the poem "Baile de La Gloria/Elegy for Manny" evokes in its retelling of the battle to save a community landmark of Westside San Antonio that used to stand at the corner of Laredo and Brazos Streets.

> Brazos, carry me there
> to that place where Tres Flores bloom ...

Brazos, carry me there
to that place where every squeeze
of the accordion

is an urgent hymn to mi raza...

Brazos, carry me across
el charco, the creek, el río—
to that place called La Gloria

The "brazos" refrain in this poem, which signifies the river of memory, the embrace of history, echoes throughout the collection with every use of the word "arms," such as the hidden stories encoded in trees and photographs. In "A Brief History of the Texas Rangers," it's "the outstretched arms of the old/álamo tree," where a Mexican husband named Genaro was lynched. It's the "odd geometry/of the cherry picker's arm," in the third poem of "A Map of Aztlan," or the "ancient bark" around which the New Man of the 20th century's "Men's Movement" wraps his tree-hugging arms. In "Song," it's the picture of starving mothers, "whose verse is brown arms/raised to the blinding sphere."

But there are other "brazos" that the poet pays homage to in these poems, such as the "too, too thin" arms of a Puerto Rican woman named Dylcia in "Destino," who climbs a Manhattan bus with her three young daughters.

Her tired, her poor: Tres hijas never cradled
In patinaed arms already filled with torch

And testament, symbol and necessity.

Although the poet sits behind Gloria Steinem on the bus, it's the poor Latina mother who signifies for him the diasporic loss that he too is experiencing in New York. And, although they ride under the myth of immigrant freedom represented by the "torch" of the Statue of Liberty, in the land that symbolizes women's liberation, Dylcia and her daughters are destined for a life of poverty and oppression.

The poet recalls his lover's arm in "Otoño," "a collar of easy warmth on my shoulders," or the "cruciate splendor" of love's surrender in "Ecclesiology" under the "fourteen stations" of the poet's kisses. In "Silk" he remembers himself as the 18-year-old having sex for the first time with an older man whose arms "wrap around [him], disappearing/ through seams, zippers, and buttons," while the "summer crickets in the yards/that bracket his car" hum steadily. In "Not There," the speaker longs for the "*T* of [his lover's] open arms, blessing me home." While in "Protocol," we see the speaker's "arms filled/with groceries and lilies from the deli" after a lover's quarrel that ends in violence and sends the poet to St. Vincent's with a "bulb of plumy flesh that would bloom in [his] eye socket."

Pain is a constant in these poems, but so is wonder, rendered in sharp lines and simple images that startle in their clarity: "a flashing congress of … fireflies," from "Wisp," for example, or, "splinters of starlight." In "Translation," the poet delights in the linguistic transformations that take place in a bilingual childhood:

> …The flowers
> that fill my sister's lace-dressed lap
>
> evolve, as if a new season of names
> just blew in: velvety cockscomb
>
> is mano de león—rooster to lion—
> and the sunset flounces of marigolds
>
> ruffle into cempasúchiles.

In "Departure," the poet's voice is "jumbo-jet/heavy," but also aware that his "father is already/hurtling toward infinity," which eases the burden of his heart and allows him the realization of his own take-off on the "runway" of his life.

His elegy to Chavela Vargas, Latina diva of song and heartbreak, is titled "La llorona," after the singer's favorite and most haunting song. In the poem, Chavela has become the iconic Weeping Woman of Mexican popular culture—a cigar-smoking "not her, not him," wailing on "bloodied knees" with her "brambled voice" for the female lover who left her.

As one of those people named in Pablo's Acknowledgments who whispered "sweet somethings" in his ear about the beauty of his poems, I am honored to write the Foreword to this heartbreakingly humble collection. What I love most about Pablo's poems, whether they are set in south Texas or Manhattan, in a museum or a movie theater or a bathhouse, is the way each one gleams off the page, the words luminous "like hundreds of tiny white moons/plucked from a brilliant Xochimilco sky," that he remembers in "After a Screening of 'María Candelaria' at the Instituto Cultural de México." And the delicate but profound insights of so many of these lines, such as the ones uttered in "The Grotto":

> Here in the wild caves we bear
> only fragile ambitions of beauty:
>
> we are born blind fish
> of blind fish...

Even as the poet honors the arms that have carried him to the "modern silence" of Appalachian nights he occupies today, in "Águila," we are carried gently into the memory of Texas as Mexico as Aztlan, its white herons, brown angels, dismembered sisters, and "the eagle/and

the serpent, an undeniable sign,/things as they were meant to be: life/
preordained, futures foretold." Until finally, all we're left with is the
halleluiah of "At the Pentecostal Baths," where in "total darkness,"

a proper businessman, yes
on his knees, imploring,
waits for ecstasy, yes.

Alicia Gaspar de Alba
January 5, 2013
Los Angeles, CA

Acknowledgments

Grateful acknowledgment is made to the following publications in which some of the poems in this book first appeared, sometimes in slightly different versions or under different titles:

Americas Review:	"Destino"
Borderlands: Texas Poetry Review:	"Chuco" and "Yours, Malinalli"
Comstock Review:	"Correspondencia" and "Vespers"
effing magazine:	"Raspado"
Gay & Lesbian Review:	"Homemakers," "Imprint," "Manhattan Triptych," and "Splash"
Gival Press (online):	"At the Pentecostal Baths"
Inkwell:	"Lights Up"
New Millennium Writings:	"The Grotto"
North American Review:	"Song" and "Yours, Sally Hemings"
QP: queer poetry (online):	"Protocol"
San Antonio Express-News:	"A Brief History of the Texas Rangers," "Allerseelen/Aztlan," "Printer's Devil," "The Saint Maker," "Summer," and "Translation"

"After a Screening of 'María Candelaria' at the Instituto Cultural de México" and "Men's Movement" were included in the anthology *Queer Codex: Chile Love* (*allgo*/Evelyn Street Press, 2004).

"Men's Movement" also appeared in *Warriors and Outlaws* (Kokopelli Publications/Dallas Poets Community, 2003).

"At the Pentecostal Baths" appeared in *Best Gay Poetry 2008* (A Midsummer Night's Press) and in *Poetic Voices Without Borders 2* (Gival Press).

Some of these poems were completed with generous support from the Alfredo Cisneros Del Moral Foundation and from the Artist Foundation of San Antonio.

Special thanks to Michael Avila, Alicia Gaspar de Alba, Lorenzo Herrera y Lozano, Karen L. Ito, Judi Nihei, Kathleen Peirce, Gloria A. Ramírez, and Debbie H. Stephens. They whispered sweet somethings in my ear. And loving gratitude to Jeanine Acquart, Francisco X. Alarcón, Francisco Aragón, Yvette Benavides, Richard Blanco, Juan Bruce-Novoa, Marisela Chávez, Mary Francine Danis, José Rubén De León, Miriam Y. Díaz, Sally Díaz Duarte, Rigoberto González, June Hankins, Ana Juárez, Michael Lueker, Roland Mazuca, Kristin Naca, Sandra M. Pérez, Ernesto Pujol, Mimi Quintanilla, Alberto Ríos, Madeline Rodríguez-Ortega, Rebecca Salazar Rush, Steve Sansom, Peter Stern, and Amy Uyematsu. They read and encouraged.

I am indebted to all the wise and beautiful poets of CantoMundo, as well as to the Macondo Writers' Workshop.

Finally, I am profoundly grateful to Sandra Cisneros and the Alfredo Cisneros Del Moral Foundation who had me fitted with a magnificent pair of wings when those accessories were in scarce supply.

Brazos,
Carry Me

You have shown me a strange image
—Plato

Toll

Listen to the tinkling
of the paletero's simple bells—

they rattle a religion deep
inside you—escúchalas

con todo tu corazón—
their song reaches heaven

long before the clang
of ponderous cathedral bronze.

I.

The Wild Caves

Wisp

I have lost my way in this
sweetgrass summer. The store clerk,

puzzled, asks if maybe the road
no longer exists. *Washed out? Detoured?*

I persist. A narrow two-lane leads past
tall mountain shadows—sprawling

ghosts—then bisects a lake, spreads
into fragrant night. A flashing congress

of tiny fireflies advertises for mates,
converses with splinters of starlight.

They point me home. *We know,*
they say. *You will be safe.* I follow.

Mohawk Reserve
Akwesasne, New York

Departure

After the burial, a trace
of Mexican sobbing.
An elderly woman, a stranger
my father's age, presses
her gnarled hand in mine
as she whispers the standard
I'm sorry for your loss,
which she follows with *I know
your heart must be heavy.*
She walks away, slowly.
How does she know this?
Heavy, yes—jumbo-jet
heavy. But like that
hump-backed oddity, also ready
to take off: the overhead
compartments shut, bags
stowed, seat-backs in the upright
position. My father is already
hurtling toward infinity—
Going home, the priest said.
I am on a runway, the lights
flashing: red, blue—
loud and lewd.

La llorona

Your brambled voice—opposite
of sumptuous—praises the wonder
of your last lover's skin, supple
as cured tobacco leaf. You grip
the cigar with practiced lips and inhale
the memory of her, then you sing:
you weep for the ceaseless work,

hard, brown; you wail for those
whose names will never be known.
And still you sing, llorona.
Your voice, a supplicant,
starts at hope and ends
in bloodied knees; darkness
always with us—viuda vestida

de luto, shuffling behind us
on crowded Mexican streets;
she is never far—in the lightless
church, and there, on the llano,
where severed limbs cling
to their thick-trunked mothers
in the windstorm—there you sing.

Your voice, Chavela—serrated
edge, shattered glass—is not heaven,
not hell; not her, not him;
your song a mouthful of sea
swallowed by the young
cliff diver—you are the sound
of love's unhealing wound.

for Chavela Vargas

Eternidad

Even as strict body counts invaded
a dream fogged by mushroom clouds
and deep-night assaults, Deborah Kerr
and Burt Lancaster surrendered

to an advancing lust that melded them
into one groping, gasping mass,
their backs sand-speckled, their bodies
glistening on a spread of beach so pure

and wide that it can't be confined
to the vast expanse of screen
at the faded movie palace
on Soledad.

Here the scene disintegrates,
their hunger atomized
into particles of dust swimming
in the projector's light,

drifting into dark, narrow places
where the truth of sex is this:
a rushed flow in the alley
behind a vacant garage, or there

in the dimly-lit park toilet, or here
in rows of stained theatre seats,
where spewed desire and petals
of torn tickets float to eternity.

Meteorology

gulfstream of sparrows
    swirls on
a weatherman's board
    autumn sky
        neatly scissored

Lights Up

It was a time of beautiful Puerto Rican men
who called you *papi* and said, *You're the one,
the only one.* And you believed, because that's how
it was back then. You followed the dazzling signs,
a blaring beat. The dreams that flared, flared
on the asphalt grid, back then, in those days
of beautiful Puerto Rican men.

It was a time of seasons, not like the ones
today. Back then, autumn meant something—
lights up, everything new: the dance, the score,
the words. And winter, well, winter was your flight
to unfurled Caribbean nights. Spring was more
and more, then summer, pouting—sigh, salt, glory.

Back then they'd call you *corazón*, and you believed—
the word switching on every goddamn light
in every goddamn chamber. They'd even call you *vida*—
vida, the skyscraper's needle, piercing the magnificence,
all the way to endlessness, back then.

Destino

The M79 cross-town bus plods, fumes, threads
Through the needle's-eye slits of Manhattan streets,

From West Side to East, conveying the old,
The devastated, the insane, the celebrated, the freshly

Ecstatic, the rest of us, happy
For the coup of an empty seat.

There is an open seat behind her—blank space
On the reverse side of this feminist icon.

I slide into place. I take a seat behind Gloria Steinem.
She is changeless: her hair still long—not cut, colored,

Or shaped by any male standard; she wears dark
Glasses—for effect or purpose, I can't tell.

Do they block out the hour's watercolored light,
Bleeding of orange into blue, garish palette that paints

The passing of another day?

At the Museum of Natural History a too, too thin
Puertorriqueña climbs on. Dylcia is her name,

Its curlicued lilt stitched on her faded uniform
In the sweatshop's early light. She shushes

Her tired, her poor: Tres hijas never cradled
In patinaed arms already filled with torch

And testament, symbol and necessity.
Las tres nenas de Dylcia cling, cry, and weave

Through the forest of multi-hued limbs
As their Mamá digs deep for change

That is never spare, change that slips through her
Slender trigueña fingers. The bus lurches. I wonder

If this route will take Dylcia and her daughters
To the same destination as the woman whose gaze

Is forward-fixed, the woman sitting just ahead.

Manhattan Triptych

1.

David Hockney in an elevator:
12, 11, 10, 9, 8,
staring straight ahead.
It's a rapidly descending
dream of blond California boys
glistening in ample pools and showers,
their beauty dispelling the Eastern gray.

2.

John Kennedy, Jr., standing
in line at the bagel shop,
Broadway and 80th—
sesame, salt, raisin, poppy. Flustered
by his radiance, the salesgirl drops
the still warm rings, letting loose
a galaxy of seeds, apologies.

3.

Leonard Bernstein in orchestra
seats at the Met. Verdi's music
uncoils in the pit. He sings along,
his crunchy basso intrusive.
No one shushes. Next to him,
a protégé, let's say, whose luster rivals
the starbursts hovering above.

The Grotto

Here in the wild caves we bear
only fragile ambitions of beauty:

we are born blind fish
of blind fish—sightless

because that first fearful one
bartered form and light for this

ceaseless calm, traded his precious
glimmer for the placid ever-dark.

The darting impulse at the sight
of hungry gar slowed to a meaningless glide.

And that other ache: all color bleached.

We dream in gray, bereft of sky-change,
time-change, and watered colors, our skins

thinned to expose a pitiable essence;
the need to sheathe effaced

when everything grazed, mated with,
nurtured by, was rendered grotesque.

Here in the wild caves our mindless wish
of eyes, pigment, modesty

drips like an icicle losing
its hold, losing itself.

Martínez

Song

after a photograph by Sebastião Salgado

The lines of the psalm follow
a starving mother across
the Sahel and another
and another, and more

who stagger on raw skin,
integument of the psalm,
pressed toward salvation
or the stark hope of it,

the mother and the psalm—
a rasp, a ripple of bone
whose mnemonic
is a stand of skeletal bark,

whose only pulse is a sky
of dumb beaks, bloody,
whose verse is brown arms
raised to the blinding sphere.

No one will hear the lines
rumble in her belly.
No one will rescue the song
clinging to her brittle lips.

Yours, Sally Hemings

All water has a perfect memory and is forever
trying to get back to where it was.
—Toni Morrison

Everything you collect,
spring buds
on the dogwood and the butterfly

that flirts with them, must be
described precisely—
named, sir.

In Paris, after those days
on a sea stirred by memory,
I walked the streets of a place

called Marais—the French name
things as they are: *Marais*, something
not quite water, not yet land.

Tonight your weight, insistent,
bears down on me. Your breath
stale. I stare at the moon,

our commonwealth, a sharp
talon ripping the dark velvet
of this difficult night.

The Birds of América: Paloma

Mourning doves scoop out
A fleshy piece of day

With their cooing—there is not
Much else to do. Tender fledglings

Are sent forth, their wings fragile
And untried. And still the cooing.

Still. The South Texas sky,
Pearly, like the inside

Of an oyster shell, has been pried
Open by a sudden, urgent flutter.

Perched high
In the palo verde,

Mourning doves coo.
There is not much else.

March 23, 2003

Translation

Heading west on Guadalupe Street
in my Dad's '56 Chevy Bel-Air,

we are mystically transfigured, block
by block: at North Trinity, Dad becomes

Papá; Mom, Mamá. We squiggly kids are niños.
Accent marks pop up at every corner, wands

that poke at the soft, doughy words
rising like warm Sunday biscuits.

We cross Zarzamora, where the Texas sun
transforms asphalt into a ribbon

of bumpy, squishy blackberry. The flowers
that fill my sister's lace-dressed lap

evolve, as if a new season of names
just blew in: velvety cockscomb

is mano de león—rooster to lion—
and the sunset flounces of marigolds

ruffle into cempasúchiles. As we near
the cemetery, el panteón, Mamá says the dead—

abuelas, abuelos, tías, tíos—are waiting
to receive la visita. She tells us this in words

that sing del allá, words that speak nuestro acá.

Allerseelen/Aztlan

Herons, the old ones say, are the ghosts
of those unable to rest. A pair of flapping,

searching souls fly beyond the Interstate:
above the steel and concrete and loud motors

and radio songs, over the spice factory,
they rise—four elegant, restless wings,

moving through feathered clouds
of canela, comino, and orégano,

scattering aromas that guide them
to a place of unsorrowed serenity.

Abuela

Streams and creeks mark the land,

insisting their way through wide terrenos—

lines and creases of abuela's hand.

Slowly she massages her rosary beads,

worn smooth as river stones—

so many prayers rippling over them.

Abuelo

Abuelo's biceps—veiny, watery,
angled by a pack of Camels—
ripple: a cool river working

at the peel of an apple.
He undresses the poem
to its pure, seed-studded core.

Some of abuelo's mottled red
lines sing long—unbroken—
curling in well-turned swirls

onto strophes of shiny linoleum;
others short: his mind darting
too quickly to form

anything longer
than a sweet,
juicy mouthful.

Tender

You hang clothes to dry in the warm promise
of summer. You ask for *horquillas*, clothespins—

the word clinging like orchids to my twelve-year-
old wishing—a soft, sexual flower, dreamed amid

hard thorns of mesquite and grass burrs. The wooden
pins dangle from your apron like stegosaurus spikes,

No. 65 in the "Dinosaurs of Our Prehistoric Earth"
album, a prize given by the attendant who flirts

with you—a stamp for every fill-up—so much
pretending as I watch, helpless, from the Buick's

backseat. Stegosaurs were herbivores: immenseness
free of meanness. How I wish we could grow plates

of armor—something to keep the brutishness away:
every day I eat spinach, you go to Mass; we pray,

with no results. But here it's just you and me—
everything fluttering, fresh: I'm free of the bully's

insults, far from his trained fist; you, safe from a slicked
desire that flaps, then folds. *Yes, ma'am, all ready to go.*

Here I am dutiful, sure—as if the things that sting
had not yet set foot on this thorny, hard-plated earth,

as if we've traveled back to a time before music was tamed,
before storms were measured, before ache had its name.

Note: In Spanish, the transitive verb *tender* means "to hang out," as clothes to dry.

Martínez

Summer

The blink, blink,
blink of lightning
bugs directs the last
flight of incoming grackles
and delayed flocks
of twittering sparrows
to their final destination.
My tía's yard is a dazzling
landing strip.

Cue

And when you say it, my heart
flutters like streamers
from rows of air conditioners
at Meyerhoff's Hardware.
My heart blasts, like the blare
from elongated brass—Renaissance
sassy—at the *palio*. When you
say it, my heart leaps
like the organ grinder's silly,
skittery monkey. At that
word, my heart is the shimmer
in schools of spring trout,
all synchronized glory. My heart—
drum-major twirl and whistle—
is alive, unlike any other,
when you utter
what I long to hear.

Ecclesiology

Splayed on our bed, your arms are cruciate splendor, blazing;
my kisses, the fourteen stations.

Your hair is loosed rays: a burst of buttresses flying, urgent,
to earth's recondite ends.

I worship here. Your offering, a slender spire reaching past
dreams of Paradise.

Your rose window seduces the heavenly light. Your back arcs,
moves heavenward—

it is the basilica's raised palate, ready to burst
with *Hosanna* and *Gloria*.

his ribs, delicate

old Gothic cathedral vaults

sources of great awe

Crime Scene

With righteous chalk
They've marked the place
Where it ended suddenly,
There on the scarred sidewalk.
A few stop to ponder and gawk
At the outline of two men
Locked in a fast embrace.

Silk

Flesh. Too much of it. More
than I can nimbly hold in my
fumbling eighteen-year-old
hand. I have never been with a man

his age, his size. That night I learn
what is meant by heavy breathing.
There is a steady hum of late
summer crickets in the yards

that bracket his car, but   .
it's the sound of his breathing
I follow, chart, and memorize.
It comes from a place overheated—

a tiny room in an old, folding
tenement—it passes through
a path, gravel-pocked,
strewn with loosened thorns.

It rings my neck, this braid
of heat and bramble and stone.
His arms wrap around me, disappearing
through seams, zippers, buttons.

There is only his industry, like Chinese
worms, feeding voraciously, exclusively,
on lush mulberry leaves, constantly
working inside their cramped cocoons:

steady motion, lissome legs—genetically
encoded—spinning, turning ceaselessly
through the warm August night.
Anatolian priests first smuggled silkworms

from China, stealing beauty they coveted,
the Turkish rug merchant explains. *See how*
expertly the silk threads are rendered invisible,
clouds whispered away. The dyer's skill

has taken a handful of summer sky, then plucked
the first rose and worked it into the border.
This is not mere craft, hakim, it is art, mastered
thoroughly. It can be yours.

Baile de La Gloria / Elegy for Manny

Brazos, carry me there,
   to that place where Tres Flores bloom
     in the warm evening breeze,

to that place where stiff petticoats
   and sleek sharkskin suits
     are the wardrobe of saints.

Brazos, carry me there,
   to that place where every squeeze
     of the accordion

is an urgent hymn to mi raza,
   and la orquesta keeps time
     to the beat of angel wings.

Brazos, carry me there,
   to that place whose canopy
     is a star-splattered San Anto sky,

to that place where love
   is pledged, and Forever
     is a promise kept.

Brazos, carry me across
   el charco, the creek, el río—
     to that place called La Gloria.

Note: La Gloria was a historically significant building in San Antonio's West Side that was, through various incarnations, a gasoline station, a dance hall, and an important site of community gathering during the first half of the twentieth century. Due to political expediency and underhandedness, La Gloria was demolished, despite community outcry, to make way for "a more economically viable" truck garage. It stood at the intersection of Laredo and Brazos Streets. "La Gloria" is also a colloquialism for Paradise.

Raspado

Texas Shaved Ice the sign reads
  an elderly couple married
    so many years they're beginning

to resemble their plump-eyed puppy
  or it could be the other way
    around they stop for a minute

well maybe five to stare at the pair
  of miniature red peafowl
    red the color of plastic Shivas

at the Dollar Store the peahen and her mate
  perched in the wispy-leafed huisache
    growing through the asphalt ballcourt

at Tenayuca High only then
  the señora and her señor order
    two raspas bright red the flavor

red a color not a fruit but
  a melting twilight sky before
    they return to their tiny house

next to the vacant lot
  a dry colorless scar
    that plot on Colorado

Correspondencia

1.

The carpenter from Vera Cruz
proudly trades a sack of green
papayas for a gram or two
of burnished prose
that will change minds
and recast his fortunes.
El jarocho's fate is sealed
with droplets of beeswax
and hope as dusk scrawls itself
across the city sky.

2.

A broken strand of yellowed pearls
is all the widow can offer
for the scribe's finest—
a letter to her son requires
elegant words and graceful turns,
which are embedded
too deep in her heart.
Like craning swans, her fingers glide
on the onionskin document
of her anticipation.

3.

In the rust-colored twilight
the scrivener's wife waits and listens
for the rattle of coins
in her husband's pockets,
a tinkling harvest gathered in the heat
and bustle of the ancient zócalo.

...

His syntax spares her
the charwoman's fate;
her pantry is a well spiced
tribute to his vocabulary.

Printer's Devil

It's one or the other, says the owner
of American Printing. *I can't hire both.*

But your ad said two, Tío reminds him.
Tío Genaro is a prize-winning pressman; my father

the best in Print Shop at Lanier High. It's 1945—
war is over and there's a bright gleam in these young

brown men's eyes—you can see it, the starburst
of possibility that swirls in them. But the owner

tells my uncle—the elder, the fixer—*just one* 'Pedro';
I don't want no trouble. As if together, my uncle, my father,

and every Chicano like them, might spill blood,
not ink. Might print feisty manifestos, instead

of hospital invoices. Might give new meaning
to "die-cut." It is 1945 and radical acts are few

in San Antonio. *Thank you, sir. My brother and I
will look elsewhere.* Tío says this even though *elsewhere*
is not much better in that oddly peaceful year.

II.

Brown Angel Pharmacy

"Je suis entre deux feux, deux véritiés, l'une à dire,
l'autre à taire."

—Jean Sénac

"No soy de aquí, ni soy de allá."

—Facundo Cabral

This Valley

This valley is filled with ghosts,
miraculous multitudes that still
the crying child and quiet restless,

aged souls, whose ghost hands till
tired earth, then harvest and sweep,
whose phantom feet memorize

labyrinths of lettuce, beet, and grape,
whose ghost throats, dry
with vineyard dust, still sing

at crimson time, whose ghost hearts
beat, though strained, whose ghost eyes
weep for what has been.

We taste their ghost work, even
praise it, but cannot see the brown
ghosts with us in this valley.

A Map of Aztlan

1. The Saint Maker (Alburquerque)

A young santero named Carrillo
whittles prayers and wishes,

and some days, tiny miracles
from the humble cedro.

With burled devotion
and his abuelo's tools he releases

Santa Bárbara and San Pedro,
San José and the Santo Niño
from their rooted wombs.

The santero carves limbs of álamo
into saints who will stand

before a mother too angry
to address God directly,

but with just enough hope
cupped in her callused palm.

Her velas almost singe, but never
singe the saints' graceful folds
of cassock and cloak. The patience

of the santero's steady hand is now
the supplicant's own. The saints hear

prayers as the saint maker listens
to voices that plead for redemption

from deep inside the perfect wood.

•

2. Chuco (El Paso)

Javier points to the everywhere
mountains: Listen to the quiet,

he says. I crane to see
the desert's jagged screams

released at the moment of its birth.
Listen to the quiet, he says. I turn

and face the mesa, long sigh of earth
expelled at its first night's dream.

A quail hen hurries her chicks
toward the acacia. Javier and I

say nothing. We listen for the quick
return of silence. We—the pinioned,

the flightless—who sleep in the tangle
of thorns, who keep watch

over each other in the curved shadow
of ram's horn, are still this day,

we are earth's warm hush as we
wait for the tenderness of rain.

•

3. Lines (Los Angeles)

High above neighborhoods of plain houses,
where hard-rain dreams of paid debts,
respect, and movie star paychecks
are unleashed in guarded brown sleep,
El Indio keeps the city's lines uncrossed,

repairs them, even reforms them,
after the stress of summer lightning—
a trick to keep us quiet: nature's plucking
the exposed guts like an overzealous
guitar player, Indio thinks. He performs

an air-guitar riff just as the odd geometry
of the cherry-picker's arm extends.
This is Indio's routine ascension.
El Indio's mind wanders, to the houses
below, and then to the lives inside.

He hovers, barely connected to earth,
and knows he is just another floating
brown skin with a job to do.
Hey, Indio, the crew boss shouts.
Git those frickin' shoes off the line.

Indio pokes at dangling soles
and yanks at tattered strings.
These were not tossed up—
El Indio says they were dropped
down by gangs of tired brown angels.

•

4. Vespers (San Antonio)

Kiko, who hears the gospel whir
   in long-vacated shells, warns his P. O.
that the chirps of angry redbirds
   are echoes of seesaws
in abandoned barrio playgrounds.
   Unsolicited info offered up
at the altar of indifference.

Kiko, who airbrushes
   twelve tattooed apostles
on the leaning wall of Mireles' garage,
   explains to the Revitalization Committee
that those vatos were also waiting
   for a second helping of grace.
Unauthorized use, the officials rule.

Kiko, whose boundaries
   are watched over by saints—
Joaquín, Felipe, Gabriel and Fernando—
   searches the West Side
for his Tepeyac, hopes
   for another vision, prays
for winter roses and rays of light.

But today he is a murmur of lint
in the pocket of a tidy god.

•

5. Ciudad Juárez

The innocence of a thousand
Juárez girls floats
at the water's edge,
where duck bills scythe unceasingly,
and a brace of egrets waits, patient,
for startled schools to reconvene.

A Full Moon Rises Over Juárez

1.
Brother, whole I am no use
to you, my head filled
with star-ashed dreams

and carefully knitted thought—
a woman's head should be a cleared
chamber, ready to humbly receive
her lord's daily bidding.

Traitor, you named me,
then made me pay the price:
my head, fount of sin,

must be severed; one swift
slash and I was shattered—
an exorbitant fling and my head
disked heavenward.

Each night, I lose more
and more, content to be
remembered; each time hoping,
hoping it will be different.

2.
Hermanos, there I was no use
to you, so I headed north,
to a land of dreams, where

my nimble fingers are prized—
their handiwork pays for new
roads, fine goats, Chinese phones.

I am a threat to brothers,
fathers, sons—a traitor,
some say. At dawn, when

the moon again fades,
erased by an eager sun,
I will join four hundred
sisters whose bones

are scattered across
this desert, our lives
scarcely remembered.

Notes:

According to Aztec mythology, Coyolxauhqui was the daughter of the Earth goddess, Coatlicue, and the sister of the Sun god, Huitzilopochtli. Coyolxauhqui encouraged her four hundred sisters and brothers to kill their mother. Coatlicue gave birth to Huitzilopochtli, who sprang out of his mother as an adult, fully armed, and saved her. To avenge his mother, Huitzilopochtli cut off Coyolxauhqui's head and threw it into the sky, where she became the Moon.

According to the National Organization for Women, for more than a decade, the city of Juárez, on the U.S.-Mexico border, has been a killing field where young Mexican women, most of whom worked in U.S.-owned maquiladoras, have been slain. It is the site of nearly 400 unsolved murders and many more abductions.

Lamento Borincano

I always believed in undressing my anguish
by simply throwing my soul to spin with the stars!
—Julia de Burgos

Imagine this: men with slicked-back hair,
obsidian sheen; they wear creamy white
jackets. You've already imagined this:
the air sweet with the perfume

of gardenia-scented women in navy
silk. They're dancing mambo
to the music of Pérez Prado.
Despreocupados. The sounds swirling.

The night, a conversation with the gods.
Imagine this too: outside the ballroom
a woman, not old, but looks so. Begs
for *un poquito* from the romancing pairs.

Asks that she be spared the potter's field—
it is her last night here, this she knows.
The poet, banished from an unfaithful earth,
will die anonymous, friendless, exiled

to nameless streets filled with cold-eyed
wanderers, far from the naranjos
of that warmer island, with only
the summer stars to eulogize her.

Imprint

don't leave
any marks
he says
polite sex
is all
a married man
allows
don't believe
his earnest
pleas, or that
he'll soon leave
his spouse, the one
who looks
for skin-
deep clues
whatever you do
don't grieve
when he says
it's over
no more
clandestine
rendezvous
you knew this
would come
but still, the sting
it pains you
to think
you didn't leave
your telling mark

Otoño

The autumn night hangs loosely
on downtown's fine-boned skyline;
we walk past the art museum,

its tall canvases and crinkled-steel
sculptures sleep, undisturbed
by the whispering, ever critical voices.

It looks like snow, I say. Your arm
a collar of easy warmth on my shoulders
as you explain away the enchantment:

It's lake effect. Just lake effect.
There's some turbulence, you tell me,
as I imagine each shimmering flake

a chip of the mirror's silver, or the shiny
scale of an overfed carp. That motion
collects warm air and creates instability,

you say, and again I am amazed
at the clash and its radiant,
evanescent results.

Protocol

The young intern at St. Vincent's didn't ask
   many questions—his shift was nearing
its eighteenth hour, and he had seen far worse
   than the bulb of plumy flesh that would bloom
in my eye socket. Besides, men do this
   kind of thing to women, not to other men.

I see, he said. My well-rehearsed speech filled
with *absent-mindedness* and *awkward hardware*.

The triage nurse, a sweet-voiced Filipino, folded
   his arms tightly. He wasn't having it. He knew. He knew.
You okay, papi? I said nothing,
   just nodded. A few tears streamed down
the acequia of my cheek. He told me not to cry,
   it would only make it worse.

A few dabs of antiseptic, some angel's-robe gauze,
a sticky bandage, and I was released. A strange way of putting it.

I'll fix a double cazuela of arroz con pollo,
   your favorite. I'll stir in a confetti of peas
and carrots. Something festive. And everything
   will be forgotten. Forgiven. Because the brutish
knot of fist unfolds, easy as dove wings, into
   the warm, fluttering caress.

I head south, my arms filled
   with groceries and lilies from the deli
on Bleecker; the melody of a Mexican bolero
   sashays in my head.

Down on Hudson Street two men scrub
  graffiti off a wall: "Die Fags," it reads.
A constellation of swastikas swirls
  around the imperative.
Crazy, ain't they, the fucks who did this,
  one of the men says as I walk past.

Yeah, crazy.

Splash

You're right, of course. Better we stay
friends, just friends—*buds,* you say.
[A bloom unopened.] Yes, let's keep it neat:
we'll leave one seat between us at the movies,
to make it clear We're Not. We're only
a couple of pals adoring their silvery idols:
Garbo, Bette—the early, the late. Yes, dear,
that gap will surely set things straight.
Tonight my hotel room was cluttered
with pining thoughts and messy wishes,
desire's detritus strewn about.
But now it's gone—all
washed away by the pool boy's
gracious "Yes, you may."

Sylvester

1.

Frère Gerbert listens to the Moors
who show him the wonder
of rounded signs, numbers

whose perfection seduces
the monk's quick mind.
He shares this splendor

with his students, young boys
who will whisper that the cleric
is a wanton heretic, but drunk

on Gerbert's sure talk of orbs
and steady motion, will dismiss
what the snide mystics preach:

the errant *religieux* can make trees
dance and cause stars to collide—
but his tables will be useless,

they insist, when the Moorish
ciphers run out, when the wayward
monk's theorems run out. The year

will end and calamity will be written
with a rigid 1 and *l'oeuves*, three
of them—three spheres trailing

the lonely one; by then Gerbert
will be called Sylvester, vicar
of the carpenter's martyred son;

Sylvester will lead his flock past
the millennium, and on to the world,
new and still spinning, old, explained,

world transformed
and deeply pained.

Note: Sylvester II, né Gerbert d'Aurillac, was the first French pope. He reigned from 999 to 1003.

2.

You make me feel, the mad queen
wails. And we follow and believe.
Tongues breach dark-fingered

hours before day's light, pleated
with envy. *You make me feel.*
Beneath the magnet spin

of a mirror ball—perfect
sphere—together
with our sweaty tribe,

we extend, harden
the sex-garlanded hour,
fevered. I will not leave

you, love. Another key
change. We feel and love
what is hidden behind

the fig leaf. We shun
the predictable ray
that whispers to the green:

Grow! Widen! No, let us keep
the light at bay. Here,
in the countdown

to a viral age—the pock-marked,
wasting hour about to dawn—
we twirl, colliding stars.

Sylvester—pulsing siren, chosen
one—lead us to the world, new
and still spinning, old, explained,

world transformed
and deeply pained.

Note: Sylvester, né Sylvester James (1948-1988), is considered a major pioneer of 1970s
and 80s disco music.

Watching the Dancers

after the photograph by Edward S. Curtis

"They wear their native dress
for the pueblo feast day,"
says the taped voice, authoritative,

later emphasizing: "This is Curtis
at his lyrical best. Notice
that the subjects, young maidens,
face away from us.
They are watching the dancers below."

But it is the young maidens' hair
that astonishes: jet-black
butterfly whorls, molded obsidian,
twisted, squash blossom style—
the atoo, says the ghost voice.

A tour group, six young Tewa girls, enters
the gallery—they wear headphones,
squash blossom style, echoes of the dear sisters.
They listen to the solemn introduction:

"Curtis' sweeping project was to document
the North American Indian,
which he labeled 'the vanishing race.'"

The Tewa girls laugh, loud, face
away from us,
and dance to the next room
at the big history museum.

Not There

Here, away from you, I miss
our silver waltzing, your anise

kisses, the way your knees bend
to admire something easily passed,

to comfort the thing amiss. Here,
I miss how you cloud my glass

of morning water, the way
you complicate the days

and pillow my pain-colored
hour. Here, the neat vines,

like lines of synchronized
ballerinas, make me long

for your mutt-in-the-truck,
let's-swallow-the-night ways.

I long for the *T* of your open
arms, blessing me home,

shooing away my empty *here*,
tuning up our brass-band *there*.

Homemakers

Same-sex marriage = heteronormative praxis!
—comment posted on Facebook
Make it new.
—Ezra Pound

When two men make a home
it is more than board
and wire and stone; it is
a puzzle, an address
for neighbors' scorn, this
the husband and husband know,
so they frame their home with care
and well-tended beds—
bearded irises, starry
corn-blues. This is how
they make it new.
These men will gripe and cook
and such, but mostly they will love—
they will love in that Genesis way,
before the hissing and the shame;
they will let music play
in formal spaces, they will stir
the breeze with uncued kisses,
then shush the night
with circles traced
on gym-tamed places.
This is what two men do
when they make a home:
they vow to crumple blueprints,
they vow to make it new.

After a Screening of "María Candelaria" at the Instituto Cultural de México

When her twisted path finally leads
to our front door, fight La Pelona off
as long as you're able—be Pedro Armendáriz

to my Dolores Del Río and tell La 'Pestosa
that it was the stones of mi gente's hatred
and the blaze of their heated intolerance

that summoned her to our chinampa. But if
she prevails, go into our jacal and find the oar
that will row me al otro lado. Lay me

in the lanchita on a cushion of serene white
poppies, like hundreds of tiny white moons
plucked from a brilliant Xochimilco sky.

Gay Pride Weekend, 2003

Movement

A young Chicano charms

a snake of shopping carts

across the asphalt sprawl—

the metal coil writhes,

a DNA of never-ending toil.

A Brief History of the Texas Rangers

Mañana, por la mañanita—
Epifania to her comadre Anita.

Tomorrow, in the little morning,
Epifania, alone, in that shrunken,

womanish hour—she alone
will lower her husband, Genaro,

into a cool, caliche-veined eternity.
Tonight she watches over him, taken down

from the outstretched arm of the old
álamo tree, lowered by strong neighbors—

Quickly! Quickly!—
young vecinos who know the night moves

with the sting of spurs and the neigh
of sweating palominos, brown

men who tell her the darkness
blooms with gunpowder

and kerosene. Epifania, alone,
rubs sábila into Genaro's thin neck,

collar of raw skin, as if the salve
might bring him back—breathing, clean.

Tonight Genaro's eyes are two frozen black stars
in the hours before the little morning.

Re-presentation

The tired widow—black wool
and unwashed hair—watches
the rapid motion above: fast-
moving clouds, long flaps of white
chenille thwumped over blue;
eager birds seduced east, away
from the sad trees and dried
grass, and in that racing
moment, she remembers...

I am the Mexica princess, presented
to the pale queen, her odd soldiers

at my side—they fear I will lunge
and pluck her regal heart. See how

she marvels at my golden cuffs,
hammered sunlight, and my pectoral,

made from the feathers of *coyotl* night.
See how she touches her Spanish cheek,

then points to mine, smooth, dark—
all her courtiers laugh and mock.

Lords, do not forsake me
in this unlearned land, far
from my priests and stones.

Lords, let these blind curs eat
the grains of knowledge;
help them see and understand.

I was the rare bird, extravagant, plumed,
that should have flown before they steered
the wooden fish to these bland, sunless shores...

A loud clatter—milk wagons, fruit
vendors, jostling children—wakes
the old widow. Flocks of common
pigeons wreathe her aching feet.

A Garden in Abiquiu

The quiet heat
of summer's afternoon
twists the flower
of jimson weed

into a knot
of white handkerchief
'til the early rain
is wrung out

bright tears
saved in folds
of perfect white

Yours, Malinalli

The signs burned my sleep
long before you arrived on snorting,
glistening spirits. One-eyed fish, spawned
in the sacred lagoon, foretold
your coming.
I whispered a prayer
into my palms and pressed them
against the temple stone.

Your red-bearded language,
sweet on my tongue, demanded
a path between my words
and yours. In the avenues
of Tenochtitlan they say
I am your whore;
the new word is stranded
in the narrow canal of my Nahuatl throat.

Águila

Against this still Appalachia night
our hearts strike a dissonant chord.
So much quiet outside the little panes.
But our bed is a complex matrix of frayed
plans and out-of-reach dreams. My parents
and your parents believed in the eagle
and the serpent—an undeniable sign,
things as they were meant to be: life
preordained, futures foretold. But you
and I are of another time: no caves,
no long trek, no cactus—no feathered
shriek, no scaled hiss to guide us—only
our modern silence and one tentative kiss.

Men's Movement

Go ahead—howl at the moon,
Hug a tree, bang the drum,
Beat your chest. Be a man
Among men. Pero oye, carnal,
As you smudge the sacred mud

On limb, on breast, on groin,
Remember the deafening howl
Of our love when first expressed.
As you wrap your arms
Around the ancient bark,

Remember the promise
That enveloped and bound us,
Tight, one to the other.
Hit mallet against taut hide
And remember the hastened beat

Of my heart as I pressed
Against you. Pound
Your smooth chest
Con tu puño de canela
And feel the sirocco de mi boca

On that perfect symmetry,
Consecrated con mis besos.
Prove your tenderness
To those men—prove it
With all your might.

Mundillo

The radiant winter moonlight
And her tranquil sisters,
December's tired branches—

Agile lace makers. This night
They tat delicate
Patterns on our patio,

Dainty and fine
As anything made
By silent Spanish nuns.

Martínez

Litanía latina

We are the ones we have been waiting for.
—Message from the Hopi Elders

Saint Tito, halo of glittering timbal,
   play for us.

Divina Celia, salsera sin igual,
   sway for us.

Blessèd Ritchie, hijo del son jarocho,
   rock and roll for us.

Santa Selena, tesoro del tejano,
   unfold your soul for us.

Revered Desiderio, conguero of the orishas,
   make a loud noise for us.

Belovèd Lola, canto ronco del norteño,
   be a proud voice for us.

Cherished Narciso, padrino del llanto obrero,
   dip and glide for us.

La Lupe querida, cubana complicada,
   burn a light for us.

All you brown saints and angels,
   sing your songs for us;
      whisper our names
         to a god who longs for us.

At the Pentecostal Baths

Tactile, yes. In total darkness, yes.
As if eclipsed. As on his lips.
As if in secret retreat,
finding his way, eagerly. Yes.

A room filled with men, yes.
Lightness years away.
He waits for the coming
of the Paraclete,

a proper businessman, yes,
on his knees, imploring,
waits for ecstasy, yes.
Glory revealed in silver-

dollar holes. Halos, yes.
Come with thy grace
and heavenly aid,
he begs.

There are no tongues
of flame. Is this
how it ends? This is
how it ends, yes.

Pablo Miguel Martínez's poems have appeared in numerous publications, including *Americas Review, Borderlands: Texas Poetry Review, BorderSenses, Comstock Review, effing magazine, Harpur Palate, Gay and Lesbian Review, Inkwell, La Voz de Esperanza, Lodestar Quarterly* (online) *New Millennium Writings, North American Review, QP: queer poetry* (online) and the *San Antonio Express-News.* His prose has been published in *El Aviso* (NALAC), and in the *San Antonio Current*, where he was a frequent contributor, as well as in the *El Paso Times* and in *La Voz de Esperanza.* His poetry has been anthologized in *Best Gay Poetry 2008* (A Midsummer Night's Press), *Poetic Voices without Borders 2* (Gival Press, 2009), *Queer Codex: Chile Love* (Evelyn Street Press, 2004), and *Warriors and Outlaws* (Kokopelli Publications/Dallas Poets Community, 2003). His work also appears in the forthcoming anthology, *This Assignment Is So Gay* (Sibling Rivalry Press, 2013). In 2009 he received the Robert L.B. Tobin Award for Artistic Excellence; in 2007 he received the Oscar Wilde Award. Pablo was awarded the prestigious Chicano/Latino Literary Prize in 2005. His literary work has also received support from the Artist Foundation of San Antonio and the Alfredo Cisneros Del Moral Foundation.

Pablo has read his work at numerous venues, including the University of Texas at Austin; Austin International Poetry Festival; McKinney Ave. Contemporary Art Center (Dallas); Katherine Anne Porter House (Kyle, TX); Painted Bride Art Center (Philadelphia); Poetry at Round Top. In San Antonio, he has read his work at Bihl Haus Gallery, Esperanza Peace and Justice Center, Gemini Ink, Our Lady of the Lake University's Poetry Festival, San Antonio Poetry Festival, San Antonio Public Library, Southwest School of Art, and Trinity University.

Pablo has taught English at Our Lady of the Lake University (San Antonio) and at Lone Star College (Houston). He holds an MFA degree in Creative Writing from Texas State University-San Marcos.

In addition to being a Founding Member of CantoMundo, a national retreat-workshop for Latina/o poets, Pablo has also participated in Sandra Cisneros' Macondo Writers' Workshop.

Currently Pablo lives in Louisville, Kentucky, with his life-partner, Henry Cantú.

OTHER KÓRIMA PRESS TITLES

Ditch Water: Poems
      by Joseph Delgado

Empanada: A Lesbiana Story en Probaditas
      by Anel I. Flores

Joto: An Anthology of Queer Xicano & Chicano Poetry
      edited by Lorenzo Herrera y Lozano

Las Hociconas: Three Locas with Big Mouths and Even Bigger Brains
      by Adelina Anthony

Tragic Bitches: An Experiment in Queer Xicana & Xicano Performance Poetry
      by Adelina Anthony, Dino Foxx, and Lorenzo Herrera y Lozano

Made in the USA
Las Vegas, NV
15 April 2023

70632818R00062